CONTENTS   UNIT 32

INTRODUCTION

This final unit of the course is in two parts. In the first part, Professor Edwin Morgan introduces the work of three contemporary East European poets, Zbigniew Herbert (Poland), Miroslav Holub (Czechoslovakia) and Vasko Popa (Yugoslavia), together with a brief selection of their poems. He suggests that they offer an illuminating 'European' perspective from which to view British writing, while the influence of Popa on Ted Hughes may be taken as representing a new 'openness' towards poetic traditions other than our own. In the second, Alasdair Clayre discusses a phenomenon affecting the poetry of the last two decades, the emergence of a 'poetry in public', often for performance, associated with the large poetry readings of the 1960s. He considers some of its sources in American poetry, the critical debate which it generated, and its connections with folksong and poetry in an oral tradition.

Alasdair Clayre is a BBC member of the course team. He has published a volume of poems *A Fire by the Sea* (1973, Compton Russell), a collection of poems and songs, *Adam and the Beasts* (1974, Faber) and a record of the same title, the songs in performance, by Acorn Records. Professor Morgan of the Department of English, Glasgow University, has published translations of several European poets, together with a version of poems by Mayakovsky into Scots entitled *Wi the Haill Voice* (1972). The most recent volume of his own poems is *From Glasgow to Saturn* (Carcanet Press, 1973).

For programmes related to this unit, see the Broadcast Notes.

THE OPEN UNIVERSITY

Arts : A Third Level Course
Twentieth Century Poetry

Unit 32

EAST EUROPEAN POETS

Prepared for the Course Team by Professor Edwin Morgan,
University of Glasgow

POETRY IN PUBLIC

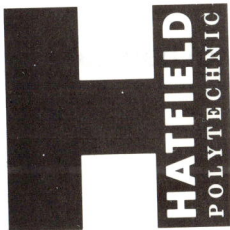

Cover   *The Tower of Babel*, etching by Michael Craig (*By courtesy of the City Gallery, Milton Keynes*).

The inscription reads:

By the Sons of Noah were the Nations divided on the Earth after the Flood, and the whole Earth was of one Language. And they found a Plain in the Land of Shinar and dwelt there saying: Let us build us a City, and a Tower whose top may reach unto Heaven, and let us make us a Name, lest we be scattered abroad upon the Face of the Earth. And the Lord came down to see the City and the Tower which the Children of Men builded. And the Lord said; Behold, the People is one, and this they begin to do, and nothing will now be restrained from them. So the Lord scattered them abroad from thence upon the Face of all the Earth, and confounded the language. Therefore is the Name of that Tower called Babel.

The Open University Press
Walton Hall, Milton Keynes
MK7 6AA

First published 1976

Designed by the Media Development Group of the Open University.

Printed in Great Britain by
EYRE AND SPOTTISWOODE LIMITED
AT GROSVENOR PRESS PORTSMOUTH

ISBN 0 335 05123 5

This text forms part of an Open University course. The complete list of units in the course appears at the end of this text.

For general availability of supporting material referred to in this text please write to the Director of Marketing, The Open University, P.O. Box 81, Walton Hall, Milton Keynes, MK7 6AT.

Further information on Open University courses may be obtained from the Admissions Office, The Open University, P.O. Box 48, Walton Hall, Milton Keynes, MK7 6AB.

1.1

CONTENTS   EAST EUROPEAN POETS

EAST EUROPEAN POETS

1   INTRODUCTION

1.1   Islanders are often accused, perhaps naturally enough, of being insular. Because Britain, from Europe's point of view, is an off-shore island with many peculiarities, Europeans often feel that we wilfully shut ourselves off from cultural influences which to them are important. It is true that it can take a surprising time for a new idea, or a new form of art, to cross the narrow strip of water that divides us from the Continent; in fact, some things never get across at all. We can defend ourselves by saying that the Continental experience is not our experience, and therefore why should we burden ourselves with material that's irrelevant to our own lives? But it seems less and less true that there is any real irrelevancy. Quite apart from the fact that we have become more involved in the affairs of Europe in recent years, I'd like to argue that we have much to learn from modern European writers, and particularly from three East European poets, Zbigniew Herbert in Poland, Miroslav Holub in Czechoslovakia, and Vasko Popa in Yugoslavia. Of course reading poems in translation is never quite the same as being in living touch with the original words, but it so happens that these three poets, because of their free verse and their usually direct language, translate well into English, with much less loss of flavour and distinctiveness than would often be the case. All three have appeared in the Penguin Modern European Poets series.

1.2   But why should we read them? One broad answer might be that they have had to produce their work under extremely testing social and political circumstances, and that this has given their poetry an edge, a clear-eyed quality not quite like anything we are familiar with in our own poetry. Another answer might lay stress on the theme of survival which in fact they do share with many Western poets but which they deal with in fresh and urgent ways because they see it from a different background, a different angle. Or from a third viewpoint, we might say that there is something to be learned from their attitude to language, from their pared-down, sinewy, anti-florid expression. Indeed, on this last point, their work was no sooner translated than it began to interest and influence British poets.

1.3   It would clearly be inadequate and improper to lump together the post-war histories of Poland, Czechoslovakia, and Yugoslavia, each of which is a country with its own marked traditions; but what these countries do share, and we do not, is an inevitable awareness of frontiers, invasions, insurrections, resistance movements, and massive and sometimes violent political change. At times it must seem to a jaundiced eye as if Europe had got stuck at the Renascence stage of the emergence of nations, tetchily blowing their trumpets and stockpiling their gunpowder. But this would be unfair, if only because the tutelary spirits of America and Russia have interfered and are interfering with the natural development of European society, for their own ends. Given autonomy, Europe could still spring surprises. However, the situation as it is reminds one of the watch tower and the customs post, the long historical memory and the precarious power bloc. So if we have *Realpolitik*, do we also have *Realdichtung*? A poetry that is pragmatically determined to survive at all costs, to assert its existence and its rights in the face of severe pressures from surrounding social and political situations? The answer to that question will best be seen if we examine the work of the three poets mentioned above.

2 ZBIGNIEW HERBERT

2.1 Zbigniew Herbert was born in 1924 and grew up under Nazi Germany's occupation of Poland. He fought in the Polish resistance in his teens. He studied law and philosophy during the oppressive Stalinist post-war years, and only began publishing the volumes of his poetry after the 'Thaw' of the mid-1950s. He is, therefore, a poet who came to his maturity in times of the utmost difficulty and dislocation, with war and politics as elements of the air – frontiers crossed, cities bombed, edicts proclaimed, art censored. Anything that one would want to call normality seemed far from his experience – except that what he experienced was in fact normal for millions of Europeans. Under circumstances like these, if there was any lesson European poets had to learn, and did learn, it was the lesson that patience, irony, deliberation, cunning, and an anti-hysterical and even anti-indignant art were more likely to make their points than a romantic or rhetorical grasping of lapels, poets' or readers'. Herbert's art is intelligent, reflective, dry. History, both modern and ancient, is there; but it has been shaken out, hung up on the line: it is shirts and dusters, rather than flags and plumes. In one poem the Longobards of the Dark Ages flock into the valley 'shouting their protracted nothing nothing nothing' ('The Longobards'). In another poem the Polish general boasts that the Germans shall not have one button, and the buttons mock that no one shall have the soldiers 'sewn flatly on to the heath' ('Farewell to September'). Of five men executed at dawn, two very young and the others middle-aged, 'nothing more/can be said about them' ('Five Men'). Even in Paradise there is a work week of thirty hours, and few see God, 'he is only for those of 100 per cent pneuma' ('Report from Paradise'). And here on earth, in contemporary Europe, fear is not the unknown or the supernatural but 'a scrap of paper/found in a pocket/ "warn Wójcik/the place on Dluga Street is hot" ' ('Our Fear').

2.2 A sense of history does pervade Herbert's work, in prose as in poetry. In a book of essays (*The Barbarian in the Garden*), themes of art or religion mingle with historical meditation. Van Gogh's Arles is traced back in history and out into a consideration of the Provençal poet Mistral and the problems of regional and national identity. Noting how certain methods used against the medieval Templars were added to the natural repertory of power and oppression: 'In history nothing is ever finally closed'. And in prehistoric Lascaux human history becomes basic in cave-paintings: 'Colours: black, bronze, ochre, vermilion, crimson, mallow, and limestone white . . . Colours of earth, blood and soot'.

2.3 This earth, blood and soot; scrap of paper; button on a soldier's blouse: all this wrung-out, dry-eyed evidence of the reality of danger and suffering and the inescapability of the socio-political order will tend to imply a certain view of the poet's function.

2.4 The poet is to be wary, precise, concrete, hard, impersonal, unlyrical, unpretentious.

> my imagination
> is a piece of board
> my sole instrument
> is a wooden stick
>
> I strike the board
> it answers me
> yes – yes
> no – no
>
> ('A Knocker')

In 'Tamarisk', the Homeric bard confesses how in his emphasis on battles and heroes and storms at sea he had forgotten the tamarisk, a 'common plant, prolific and useless', cousin perhaps to Robert Graves's common asphodel – the tough, unscented reality that lies at the heart of both history and poetry. The poet strikes the plain bit of board, remembers the dry twig of the tamarisk, praises a simple pebble because it is 'mindful of its limits' and 'cannot be tamed', humorously strokes an oaken stool because it is 'genuine'. It is almost as if life had taught the poet no longer to trust anything beyond immediately tangible objects and necessities, above all not to trust the heroic gesture, the flamboyant claim, the fanatical or obsessional path. To survive, even unheroically, may be the heroism of our times. The emphasis on ordinary things may strike a chord in the mind of readers who have heard the German poet Rilke exclaim in his ninth *Duino Elegy*:

> Are we, perhaps, *here* just for saying: House,
> Bridge, Fountain, Gate, Jug, Fruit tree, Window, –
> possibly: Pillar, Tower?. . . . but for *saying*, remember,
> oh, for such saying as never the things themselves
> hoped so intensely to be.
>
> (Trans. J. B. Leishman)

But there is a big difference between Rilke's marshalling of 'die Dinge' into what are eventually huge symbolic and aesthetic constructs, and Herbert's anti-aesthetic insistence on the plain irreducible fact.

2.5 In 'Jonah', where he retells the biblical story from his own point of view, it is very characteristic that he concentrates on the latter and less well-known part of the legend, Jonah's second journey, after he has been saved out of the whale's belly. Whereas the biblical Jonah hastens to obey God's second command to go to Nineveh and prophesy doom against that wicked city, Herbert's Jonah is once bitten twice shy:

> saved
> he behaves more cleverly
> than his biblical colleague
> the second time he does not take on
> a dangerous mission
> he grows a beard
> and far from the sea
> far from Nineveh
> under an assumed name
> deals in cattle and antiques

2.6 This Jonah has had enough dangerous missions; he has come through the hell of the whale's belly and now he would settle for a little private life. The disguised appearance, the change of environment, the new name and occupation, the attempt to find a new and unfanatical life, all reflect the European experience which Herbert starts off from. Like many East European poets, he uses figures from history and legend in parable contexts where their story is retold with a twist that forces attention on unexpected implications.

2.7 In another poem he takes up the Greek legend of the flaying of Marsyas by Apollo. In the original story – one of the most striking and horrible of the Greek legends – Marsyas had challenged Apollo, as the god of music and poetry, to a musical contest: the gods judged Apollo the winner, and to celebrate his success he bound Marsyas to a tree and flayed him of his whole skin, leaving him howling on the tree. Herbert, unlike the gods, is pro-Marsyas, and shows Apollo as an icy perfectionist with 'nerves of artificial fibre'.

> shaken by a shudder of disgust
> Apollo is cleaning his instrument

Apollo walks away from the scene, along a formal path 'hedged with box', while the very foliage of the tree Marsyas is tied to turns white. Marsyas becomes a general symbol of human suffering, but especially the suffering that comes at the hands of cruel or arbitrary power. He is like Prometheus on his rock. And as Shelley in *Prometheus Unbound* extracted hope from the endurance of that sufferer, Herbert in his 'Apollo and Marsyas' sees hope that the apparently monotonous brute-like howl of pain from Marsyas will some day evolve into a far more rich and far more fully human music than the ideal harmonies of Apollo:

> a new kind
> of art – let us say – concrete

'Concrete', because it will come out of the whole reality and pain of history, and also because (like Herbert's own art) it will deal in concrete particulars, defined images, precise movements of thought, unpompous deployments of vocabulary.

2.8 On the latter point, one of the results of Herbert's concrete, controlled, anti-diffuse attitude to language is his fondness for the prose poem. Often regarded as a rather suspect form, neither fish nor flesh, the prose poem can in the right hands be an admirable medium for concentrated effects. Here is one example:

From Mythology

First there was a god of night and tempest, a black idol without eyes, before whom they leaped, naked and smeared with blood. Later on, in the times of the republic, there were many gods with wives, children, creaking beds, and harmlessly exploding thunderbolts. At the end only superstitious neurotics carried in their pockets little statues of salt, representing the god of irony. There was no greater god at that time.

Then came the barbarians. They too valued highly the little god of irony. They would crush it under their heels and add it to their dishes.

What is particularly interesting in this prose poem is the economy with which irony is used to present the subject – which is itself irony. In an effete, overblown civilization which has gone through all the phases of worship, no straightforward belief would bring anything but a yawn – there is nothing but irony left, and even that (potent though it is) is not to be crudely worshipped in the old way except by the superstitious. At that stage the culture is ripe for barbarian invasion and takeover. A new irony then emerges: the barbarians are pragmatists who enjoy the turn of the wheel, sophisticates down primitives up, and they laugh robustly at the irony which has allowed them to overthrow the old god of irony.

2.9 One of Herbert's best-known poems also happens to be one which brings together many of the ideas that have been discussed. 'Elegy of Fortinbras' is a very 'European' poem in the sense that Fortinbras has never seemed such an interesting character to poets and critics inside Britain as he does to those on the Continent. '*Hamlet* without the prince' is our cliché for anything that lacks its one essential element, yet it is not hard to see how important Fortinbras is, looked at from a slightly unfamiliar angle, that is from an interest in political and historical change. We have become so obsessed by the idea of *Hamlet* as an *inward* play, a play about conscience or the ethics of revenge, or suicide, or madness, or role-playing and antic dispositions, that it comes to us with a shock to go through the text carefully and observe how much of the drama is devoted to political matters, to Denmark and its neighbour countries, to the succession and Hamlet's hopes in it, to the possibilities of invasion, to treaties, to national character, to war and soldiering and conceptions of military honour. Our critics show what to Europeans must seem a genius in skating over the very strange fact that when Hamlet dies his country is calmly handed over to an alien Norwegian freebooter, Fortinbras, who may indeed be a prince but who is described earlier in the play as having 'sharked up a list of lawless resolutes' to invade Denmark, and when this proves abortive, is on his way back from successfully attacking Poland when the Danish crown falls into his lap without a struggle.

2.10   Herbert, from his Polish vantage point, sees the fascination of this aspect of *Hamlet* – *Hamlet* as a European play, a play about frontiers, about rule and policy and ambition – and writes his poem as a dramatic monologue from Fortinbras, the one who at the end of the débâcle comes out on top. Addressing the dead Hamlet, Fortinbras speaks as the man of action who is willing to give him a military funeral because that is the only ritual he knows:

> You will have a soldier's funeral without having been a soldier
> the only ritual I am acquainted with a little
> There will be no candles no singing only cannon-fuses and bursts
> crepe dragged on the pavement helmets boots artillery horses
>   drums drums I know nothing exquisite
> those will be my manoeuvres before I start to rule
> one has to take the city by the neck and shake it a bit

To Fortinbras, Hamlet 'believed in crystal notions not in human clay'; he was 'not for life', and although he accomplished what he had to accomplish, it was an accomplishment in the realm of death, 'but what is heroic death compared with eternal watching'. Fortinbras and Hamlet are perhaps both heroic, but whereas Hamlet knows about this majestical roof fretted with golden fire, Fortinbras knows about frontiers. Fortinbras's case is put as the case of a vigilant man who will see how to rule, and do it. His limitations are clear, even to himself, but Herbert is writing at a time and in a world where survival has pushed itself up in the scale of values and tragic heroism has slipped down. This gives an edge of sympathetic understanding to the portrait, even while the man's bluntness and embryo ruthlessness might make us despair of a society composed of Fortinbrases.

> Adieu prince I have tasks a sewer project
> and a decree on prostitutes and beggars
> I must also elaborate a better system of prisons
> since as you justly said Denmark is a prison
> I go to my affairs This night is born
> a star named Hamlet We shall never meet
> what I shall leave will not be worth a tragedy

This is beautifully poised, and the balance between the incongruous extremes of 'a sewer project' and 'a tragedy' – both of them excellent things – has something about it that is typical of Herbert and his wry, ironical probing of both life and art.

3 MIROSLAV HOLUB

3.1 Miroslav Holub, born in 1923, is an almost exact contemporary of Zbigniew Herbert, and as a Czech he has lived through times only marginally less disruptive and difficult than those of Herbert's experience in Poland. His career, however, has been quite different. He studied medicine, and became a distinguished pathologist. He has done research in Germany and America as well as in his own country, and he has edited a popular science magazine. And it's perhaps of special interest here in the West, where we have suffered in our thinking in the twentieth century from a split between the sciences and the arts, and where many of our poets and critics have been deeply suspicious of science and technology and all their works, to look at a writer like Holub. He can make us examine attitudes that may be too blandly held. As he has said himself: 'Superstitious exclusion of science from arts and humanities does not preserve creativity; it preserves only old approaches and old reactions.' (Quoted in the introduction to the Penguin *Selected Poems*, p 16.)

3.2 In his poetry, his scientific training will sometimes show in a very precise use of vocabulary, including technical terms where they seem necessary ('hypertension therapy', 'paper electrophore', 'the greenish-blue pool of the chromatogram', 'the stars were taking in/signals on a frequency of ten megacycles'). Highly specialized words are sparingly used, however, and the context generally helps to explain them. In the main, what Holub wants is to remind his readers from time to time that they are living in a world where science raises important and fundamental questions. It is also a world where the scientist must sometimes question himself and his activity. In a poem called 'Suffering', Holub takes up the subject of biological research, and in particular the pain and death it causes to animal species lower than ourselves in the evolutionary scale. What might be in other contexts a cliché of vivisection polemic becomes in his hands a moving presentation of a very deep dilemma – a real one because the author has been through it himself many times. He deliberately pulls the chair out from sentiment by writing about ugly, unnamed, absurd-looking microscopic creatures with bristles on their bottoms, describes how they are cut up and killed, and then makes his point:

> Naturally no one asks
> Whether these creatures wouldn't have preferred
>   to live all in one piece,
>   their disgusting life
>   in bogs
>   and canals,
> Whether they wouldn't have preferred to eat
>   one another alive,
> Whether they wouldn't have preferred to make love
>   in between horror and hunger,
> Whether they wouldn't have preferred to use
>   all their eyes and pores to perceive
>   their muddy stinking little world

Nothing about the creatures and their lives seems attractive to us – only to them! And that is the basic worry that recurs to Holub, the ancient worry of ends and means, the sacrifice of the lesser for the greater good (we *suppose*). In a striking image in the same poem he watches how

           truth advances
like some splendid silver bulldozer
in the tumbling darkness

– silvery like some fine instrument, but a bulldozer all the same.

3.3   Concern for life is a characteristic of Holub and his poetry. Although as a scientist
      he must search for ways of bettering the human condition, he never forgets the
      stubborn realities, the bedrock human evidence. A poem called 'Death in the
      Evening' describes the death of a woman in a house, but then goes on:

          But towards midnight
          the dead woman got up,
          put out the candles (a pity to waste them),
          quickly mended the last stocking,
          found her fifty nickels
          in the cinnamon tin
          and put them on the table,
          found the scissors from behind the cupboard,
          found a glove
          they had lost a year ago,
          tried all the door handles,
          tightened the tap,
          finished her coffee,
          and fell back again.

          In the morning they took her away.
          She was cremated.
          The ashes were coarse
          as coal.

      The final image in a defence of ordinariness, of an almost instinctive human care
      and persistence. The human fibre may be coarse, but it's coarse like coal: and light
      and heat will come from it sooner or later. It is noticeable again in this poem how what
      could become a troublesome sentimentality is kept at bay by the fantasy of the acts
      of the dead woman. She did not in fact do these things, she was lying dead in the
      normal mild chaos of a lived-in house, but these are the things she would have done
      if any warning of her death had been given her. These are how her love – practical,
      immediate, 'coarse' if you like – would have shown itself.

3.4   What is distinctive in Holub is that he's conscious of this endlessly persistent, strug-
      gling life wherever it's to be seen, whether it's in the room of a dying woman or on the
      slide of a microscope. This, perhaps, is where the scientist enters the picture, observing,
      noting, finding analogies. At the analogy stage, the scientist becomes the poet, the
      man of imagination. Here is a short poem which illustrates this process.

      In the Microscope

      Here too are dreaming landscapes,
      lunar, derelict.
      Here too are the masses
      tillers of the soil.
      And cells, fighters
      who lay down their lives
      for a song.

Here too are cemeteries,
fame and snow.
And I hear murmuring,
the revolt of immense estates.

There is an unusual ability to realize that although human beings see themselves as unique, and uniquely qualified to guard a central place in the ecosystem, they and their world are also a battlefield for minute forms of life, often parasitic – as we ourselves might be parasitic on creatures inconceivably large.

3.5   How then, if at all, does Holub see life advancing? He seems to settle for a wary, wily, long-term endeavour, full of mistakes and dangers, but nevertheless an increasingly conscious process, something which it is in man's nature to do, and not a divine or an accidental working-out of things. He puts this rather neatly in a tiny poem:

A Helping Hand

We gave a helping hand to grass –
    and it turned into corn.
We gave a helping hand to fire –
    and it turned into a rocket.
Hesitatingly,
cautiously,
we give a helping hand
to people,
to some people . . . . . .

(Note   The dots are Holub's.)

Holub brings us a sympathetic, imaginative, non-dogmatic humanism. It is expressed in a sculpted, tense, slightly patterned free verse that seems highly successful (as his own readings show) in combining intellectual content and the tone of a speaking voice. It is in many ways a modest poetry, but it can come across with great strength and authority. Like Herbert, Holub has had to find tightrope ways of distilling the critical essence of his life and times. Like Herbert's, his style accommodates itself readily to irony. For all his accuracy of observation and sharpness of image, he moves in his more complex poems towards ambiguity and obliquity. Significantly, one of his books is called *Although*, a title one can think of as a dialectic signal coming naturally from a poet with a materialist and Marxist background, where a questioning 'although' will often deliberately replace an accepting 'because' in order to show the potential or necessity of change. Yet Holub will also use it as the last word of a poem, followed by the three dots that invite freewheeling rather than dialectical meditation. He has himself said, however, that he has no desire to be obscure, and certainly no desire to become over-involved in the too-clever potential of irony and satire. He avoids obscurity mainly by keeping a degree of personal detachment or distancing from the concerns of the poem – what he calls his 'hard-centred approach to poetry'. The poet, as he sees it, is not *in* his poem. He will often use parable or fable, in order to dramatize, to suggest, to draw parallels. And this can work either through wit and humour or with powerful, controlled emotion, as two examples might show.

3.6   'Brief Thoughts on Cracks' is exactly what its title says it is, except that it continually invites the reader to interpret what it is saying, in terms of human behaviour, moral, social, and above all political. As the poem points out, almost everything is liable to crack sometime – an egg, armour, a book's spine. But cracks tend to be repaired, no one likes to see a crack. And if not repaired, well then, we pretend there's no crack, the cracks are all 'talked out of existence'. Ah, but then –

> But a mended egg is no longer an egg,
>   soldered armour is no longer armour,
>   a bandaged heel is an Achilles heel and
>   a man talked out of existence is not the man he was
>   rather the Achilles heel of others.
>
> Worst of all is when hundreds of mended eggs
>   pass themselves off as best eggs and hundreds
>   of suits of soldered armour as true armour,
>   thousands of cracked people as monoliths.
>
> Then it's all one huge crack.
>
> All we can do in the world of cracks is
>   now and then to call out, Mr Director, mind your
>   step on the stairs,
>   you have a crack, sir, if I may say so.

The political implications of the last paragraph, and of the last line of the second paragraph, are immense, but they are not forced, and they are not specific. The reader rocks in the eggshell of a fantasy, a tale of a tub. It is merely amusing, is it not? A face cracks when it smiles.

3.7 In 'Bullfight', one of the best of his poems, Holub again, though in a more obviously serious way, makes the verse reverberate beyond its subject matter.[1] He does not stop at a feeling of human revulsion against bullfighting. There is strong emotion in the poem, but it's an emotion distinct from Holub's feeling (earlier referred to) for animals and animal suffering. It's rather the suggestion that the bull in the poem is a *person*:

> Someone runs about,
>   someone scents the wind,
>   someone stomps the ground, but it's hard.

This someone, or everyone, somewhere or everywhere, is in a state of bewildered pain, blood streaming down his back, 'tongue stuck out to the roots' (like both bull and horse in Picasso's *Guernica*), desperately trying to speak a last message:

> And then someone (blood-spattered, all in)
>   stops and shouts:
>   Let's go, quit it,
>   let's go, quit it,
>   let's go over across the river and into the trees,
>   let's go across the river and into the trees,
>   let's leave the red rags behind

But there is no escape. The red rags of the world cannot be left behind. 'Someone' is being played with and destroyed by forces he cannot yet understand. The tragedy

[1]The poem is quoted in full in the Broadcast Notes for Television Programme 15, *Miroslav Holub*.

is not in the pain and the death but in the ignorance which makes it impossible to give these things meaning, or to avoid or overcome them:

> the black-and-red bull is going to fall
> and be dragged away,
> and be dragged away,
> and be dragged away,
>
> without grasping the way of the world,
> without having grasped the way of the world,
> before he has grasped the way of the world.

Holub's careful art shows in the contrast between the heavy ritualistic repetitions of 'and be dragged away', which enact the slow dragging of the body, and the varying near-repetitions of the three final lines, which project present, past and future – with a sort of residual minimal optimism left for the very last, in the faint potential of one day being able to grasp the way of the world.

4 VASKO POPA

4.1 Vasko Popa, born in Yugoslavia in 1922, belongs to the same generation as Herbert and Holub. His educational background is more literary than theirs, as his career has been also. He is a graduate in French and Yugoslav literature, and works as editor in a publishing house. Growing up, as Herbert and Holub did, during the European devastations of the war, he shares many of their preoccupations – with history, with legend, with the basics of human behaviour – and has evolved a style that in its unindulgent economy and sinewy hardness often runs parallel to theirs, though it has its own features too, derived from folk poetry and from surrealism.

4.2 Popa has expressed his views about poetry and the poet's function in lectures and articles, and some of his comments are worth quoting. In an article published in the Italian review *La Battana* (no. 15, 1968) he emphasized the rootedness, the strange naturalness, the inspired impersonality of poetry, with the poet as a necessary but self-effacing intermediary, almost a nutrient medium in and through which poetry can grow – and it can grow nowhere else. He used a series of organic images to bring out these ideas, and in this deep sense of the organic – reminiscent at times of the 'deep image' conceptions in recent American poetry – lies perhaps the chief difference between Popa and the other two poets we have been examining. He said in that article:

> They ask what your poetry means. Why don't they ask the apple-tree
> what its fruit means – the apple? Probably if the apple-tree could speak
> it would reply: 'Sink your teeth into the apple, and you'll see what it
> means!' . . . They ask you how you have come to create poetry. Why

don't they ask the rock how it has created the gem or the bird the
fledgling or the woman the child?. . . . Without self-obliteration there is
no concentration, without concentration there is no inspiration, without
inspiration there is no revelation, without revelation there is and can
be no poetry. . . . After you have composed poetry, where is your post?
Certainly not within poetry: fancy finding in the apple the grains of
the earth that nourished it! Maybe your post is behind poetry? No, not
there either: your shadow would fall on poetry and confuse it. Under
poetry, deep under it, that is your post: like every other fostering-ground.[2]

4.3   Popa favours sequences of short poems collected around themes, rather than long
poems or separate short poems. Some of these sequences are fairly straightforward –
poems on animals or plants. Some are less straightforward than they might seem – a
series of 'Landscapes' which are set not in the world of nature but in an ashtray,
on a table, on a hat-stand, on a hand. Others devote themselves to something

Vasko Popa (Photo: Horst Tappe. Courtesy Anvil Press Poetry)

definite enough – games, bones, pebbles, suns, a box – but use the subject as starting
point for wide-ranging, at times humorous, at times 'black', ironical, or savage
explorations of human experience. And in one book-length sequence, *Earth Erect*,
he covers the history of Serbia, though it is a flashing mosaic of fact and legend in
which, as with other sequences, a great deal more is said than can be summed up in
a descriptive phrase.

[2]My own translation from the Italian. E.M.

17

4.4 At the simplest level, as in the following short piece, the observing eye of the poet picks out the shock of fatal pain and clamps it down on the page:

Pig

Only when she felt
The savage knife in her throat
Did the red veil
Explain the game
And she was sorry
She had torn herself
From the mud's embrace
And had hurried that evening
From the field so joyfully
Hurried to the yellow gate

More typical are the macabre 'Games'. In one, 'The Nail', people enact 'nail', 'pincers', and 'workmen': nail has his head pulled off by pincers, and the workmen break pincers to bits and throw him out of the window. In another, 'Ashes', people play at nights and stars: each night sets its star on fire and dances round it, some nights taking the parts of stars till only one is left, both night and star, for self-immolation. It will come as no surprise that Ted Hughes is one of Popa's admirers, and has written the introduction to the Penguin selection of his poems. The surreal cruelties, the sinister creatures, the 'universe of grim evil' as Hughes calls it, the 'simple animal courage of accepting the odds' for which he praises Popa – all these could be found in Hughes himself. And indeed his introduction is less than helpful, if you are looking for objective and specific pointers to what Popa is doing. 'His words test their way forward, sensitive to their own errors, dramatically and intimately alive, like the antennae of some rockshore creature feeling out the presence of the sea and the huge powers in it.' This is a good description of how a Hughes poem might work, but is it true of Popa?

4.5 This element of the gruesome and the horrific – and there is nothing in the 'Games' that is untrue to the actual European experience of the war and its aftermath – is presented with a good deal of irony, in accordance with the depersonalized conception Popa has of poetry. The irony comes with the fantasy, with the 'play' of ideas and images that goes back through surrealism into the magical and often incongruous juxtapositions of folk art. A rich imagination is at work in a series of 'Once upon a time' poems – parables for modern folk, perhaps. 'Once upon a time there was a number . . .', 'Once upon a time there was a mistake . . .', 'Once upon a time there was a triangle . . . .'

Once upon a time there was a triangle
It had three sides
The fourth it hid
In its glowing centre

By day it would climb to its three vertices
And admire its centre
By night it would rest
In one of its three angles

– and this 'wise triangle' proves to be self-renewing because although it keeps losing its three sides it is careful to guard the mysterious fourth, from which it regenerates itself by a sort of fission process. No implications are spelt out, but all these parable poems are filled with provocative philosophical suggestion. We are made to think of the nature of reality, the place of illusion and of imagination, the projectability of the abstract into the concrete, the nature of perfection and imperfection, symmetry and asymmetry.

4.6 The 'little box' sequence may come nearest to conventional symbolism in its comments on the relation between the individual life and the world, though even here, paradox is never very far away. In 'The Little Box' we are told how the baby box grows and grows until the cupboard it was in is now inside it, and eventually the world it was in is also inside it, but then:

> The little box remembers her childhood
> And by most great yearning
> Becomes a little box again
>
> Now inside the little box
> Is the whole world tiny small
> It's easy to put in your pocket
> Easy to steal easy to lose
>
> Take care of the little box

4.7 Popa's fondness for sequences of short poems enables him to build up some remarkable dramatic effects, where without having the clarity that a long continuous narrative form would give him, he nevertheless makes strong urgent gestures towards basic human relationships, love and hate, growth and decay, identity and union. Two such sequences in particular make their presence felt. *One bone to another* has two bones speaking, in short phrases not unlike those of the tramps in *Waiting for Godot*, about how glad they are to have got rid of the flesh, wondering what they should do with their new freedom, lie in the sun or make love perhaps, or wait fearfully for dogs, or wander over the earth – till at the end they are fused together, fused and confused in 'an ugly dream of dust', turned into the seeds of an endlessly renewed ferocious life:

> Can you hear me
> I can hear both you and myself
> There's a cockspur crowing out of us

4.8 In the other sequence, *Give me back my rags*, the speaker does everything in his power to drive off and exorcise a love-figure that haunts him. The 'rags' he wants back are his earlier hopes and dreams, all the garishly patterned stuffs of his desire and foreboding, his smiles and glances. The other figure is a 'monster', a 'dissembler' hiding behind a white scarf. Somehow the speaker must escape her clutches, and almost persuades himself he can become disembodied enough to do so:

> And you want us to love one another
>
> You can shape me from my ashes
> From the débris of my guffawing
> From my leftover tedium
>
> You can gorgeous
>
> You can seize me by the hair of forgetting
> Embrace my night in an empty shirt
> Kiss my echo
>
> Well you don't know how to love

The poems in this sequence use a nightmarish exaggerative fantasy ('my eyes will start snarling at you', 'I'll cut off your singing nails', 'Enough chattering violets enough sweet trash') to pile up feelings of desperation which are in one sense harsh and convincing but at the same time are not devoid of self-consciousness and wit.

4.9 *Earth Erect* is an impressive work on a larger scale. Called by Ted Hughes 'a celebration of Vasko Popa's national roots', it is also, as its translator Anne Pennington points out, a poem to be read on many levels, of which the national/historical may not even be the most important. History here, she says, is 'intertwined with legend; mythological, alchemical and Christian symbolism are all exploited'. The force of its symbolism can be seen in the poems dealing with St Sava, Serbia's patron saint. This thirteenth century religious and national leader is portrayed as a shepherd not of sheep but of wolves, since wolves traditionally represented the Serbs, and this startling displacement is meat and drink to the poet, as can be illustrated from the following piece:

> *St Sava's Forge*
>
> From the besieged hills
> The wolves call him
> Their backbones ablaze
>
> He stretches out his serpent-headed staff
> That they may crawl
> Peacefully to his feet
>
> He bathes them in the hot blood
> Of the holy ancestral metal
> And dries them with his red beard
>
> He forges them new backbones
> Of young iron
> And sends them back to the hills
>
> With endless howling
> The wolves greet him
> From the top of the liberated hills

The wolves appear again, surrealistically mounted on black chargers like figures in a Bosch painting, in a poem devoted to a later national hero, Black George, assassinated in 1817 by being beheaded as he slept. The 'black' of his name becomes a key-word in the elegy, as the dead man awakes (like the dead woman in Holub's poem) and goes in search of his head; the wolves ride out to meet him, and will carry his head 'On crossed black flutes/Bound with widows' black braids', and the head will shine 'Crowned with black beams/Of the black sun'.

4.10 As the sequence moves towards the present, the pilgrim figure who has recounted it all returns to his native Belgrade, at the meeting place of the sacred rivers Sava and Danube, where the wolf tracks have safely led him. The last poem is written in praise of Belgrade, the 'white city', white as a bone guarded by the sun in a golden reliquary. The religious imagery, naive yet not naive, suggests both the bold simplicity of folk art and the much more conscious modern awareness of war-devastated capital cities which can be burnt to ashes, with nothing but the bare bones of walls left standing, and still rise again.

Belgrade

White bone among the clouds

You arise out of your pyre
Out of your ploughed-up barrows
Out of your scattered ashes

You arise out of your disappearance

The sun keeps you
In its golden reliquary
High above the yapping of centuries

And bears you to the marriage
Of the fourth river of Paradise
With the thirty-sixth river of Earth

White bone among the clouds
Bone of our bones

Popa, like Herbert and Holub, shows us how much can be done with a concentrated, laconic style; with an eye on the object rather than on the poet's heart; and with a stark first-hand awareness of the dislocations, reverses, and tough hopes of life.

A SELECTION OF POEMS

ZBIGNIEW HERBERT

Report from Paradise

In paradise the work week is fixed at thirty hours
salaries are higher prices steadily go down
manual labour is not tiring (because of reduced gravity)
chopping wood is no harder than typing
the social system is stable and the rulers are wise
really in paradise one is better off than in whatever country

At first it was to have been different
luminous circles choirs and degrees of abstraction
but they were not able to separate exactly
the soul from the flesh and so it would come here
with a drop of fat a thread of muscle
it was necessary to face the consequences
to mix a grain of the absolute with a grain of clay
one more departure from doctrine the last departure
only John foresaw it: you will be resurrected in the flesh

not many behold God
he is only for those of 100 per cent pneuma
the rest listen to communiqués about miracles and floods
some day God will be seen by all
when it will happen nobody knows

As it is now every Saturday at noon
sirens sweetly bellow
and from the factories go the heavenly proletarians
awkwardly under their arms they carry their wings like violins

Our Fear

Our fear
does not wear a night shirt
does not have owl's eyes
does not lift a casket lid
does not extinguish a candle

does not have a dead man's face either

our fear
is a scrap of paper
found in a pocket
'warn Wójcik
the place on Dluga Street is hot'.

our fear
does not rise on the wings of the tempest
does not sit on a church tower
it is down-to-earth

it has the shape
of a bundle made in haste
with warm clothing
provisions
and arms

our fear
does not have the face of a dead man
the dead are gentle to us
we carry them on our shoulders
sleep under the same blanket

close their eyes
adjust their lips
pick a dry spot
and bury them

not too deep
not too shallow

A Knocker

There are those who grow
gardens in their heads
paths lead from their hair
to sunny and white cities

it's easy for them to write
they close their eyes
immediately schools of images
stream down from their foreheads

22

my imagination
is a piece of board
my sole instrument
is a wooden stick

I strike the board
it answers me
yes – yes
no – no

for others the green bell of a tree
the blue bell of water
I have a knocker
from unprotected gardens

I thump on the board
and it prompts me
with the moralist's dry poem
yes – yes
no – no

Pebble

The pebble
is a perfect creature

equal to itself
mindful of its limits

filled exactly
with a pebbly meaning

with a scent which does not remind one of anything
does not frighten anything away does not arouse desire

its ardour and coldness
are just and full of dignity

I feel a heavy remorse
when I hold it in my hand
and its noble body
is permeated by false warmth

– Pebbles cannot be tamed
to the end they will look at us
with a calm and very clear eye

Apollo and Marsyas

The real duel of Apollo
with Marsyas
(absolute ear
versus immense range)
takes place in the evening
when as we already know
the judges
have awarded victory to the god

bound tight to a tree
meticulously stripped of his skin
Marsyas
howls
before the howl reaches his tall ears
he reposes in the shadow of that howl

shaken by a shudder of disgust
Apollo is cleaning his instrument

only seemingly
is the voice of Marsyas
monotonous
and composed of a single vowel
Aaa

in reality
Marsyas relates
the inexhaustible wealth
of his body

bald mountains of liver
white ravines of aliment
rustling forest of lung
sweet hillocks of muscle
joints bile blood and shudders
the wintry wind of bone
over the salt of memory
shaken by a shudder of disgust
Apollo is cleaning his instrument

now to the chorus
is joined the backbone of Marsyas
in principle the same A
only deeper with the addition of rust

this is already beyond the endurance
of the god with nerves of artificial fibre

along a gravel path
hedged with box
the victor departs
wondering
whether out of Marsyas' howling
there will not some day arise
a new kind
of art – let us say – concrete

suddenly
at his feet
falls a petrified nightingale

he looks back
and sees
that the hair of the tree to which Marsyas was fastened
is white
completely

From Mythology

First there was a god of night and tempest, a black idol without eyes, before whom they leaped, naked and smeared with blood. Later on, in the times of the republic, there were many gods with wives, children, creaking beds, and harmlessly exploding thunderbolts. At the end only superstitious neurotics carried in their pockets little statues of salt, representing the god of irony. There was no greater god at that time.

Then came the barbarians. They too valued highly the little god of irony. They would crush it under their heels and add it to their dishes.

Elegy of Fortinbras
for C.M.

Now that we're alone we can talk prince man to man
though you lie on the stairs and see no more than a dead ant
nothing but black sun with broken rays
I could never think of your hands without smiling
and now that they lie on the stone like fallen nests
they are as defenceless as before The end is exactly this
The hands lie apart The sword lies apart The head apart
and the knight's feet in soft slippers

You will have a soldier's funeral without having been a soldier
the only ritual I am acquainted with a little
There will be no candles no singing only cannon-fuses and bursts
crepe dragged on the pavement helmets boots artillery horses drums drums
    I know nothing exquisite
those will be my manoeuvres before I start to rule
one has to take the city by the neck and shake it a bit

Anyhow you had to perish Hamlet you were not for life
you believed in crystal notions not in human clay
always twitching as if asleep you hunted chimeras
wolfishly you crunched the air only to vomit
you knew no human thing you did not know even how to breathe

Now you have peace Hamlet you accomplished what you had to
and you have peace The rest is not silence but belongs to me
you chose the easier part an elegant thrust
but what is heroic death compared with eternal watching
with a cold apple in one's hand on a narrow chair
with a view of the ant-hill and the clock's dial

Adieu prince I have tasks a sewer project
and a decree on prostitutes and beggars
I must also elaborate a better system of prisons
since as you justly said Denmark is a prison

I go to my affairs This night is born
a star named Hamlet We shall never meet
what I shall leave will not be worth a tragedy

It is not for us to greet each other or bid farewell we live on archipelagos
and that water these words what can they do what can they do prince

Practical Recommendations in the Event of a Catastrophe

It usually begins innocently enough with an acceleration, un-noticeable at
first, of the turning of the earth. Leave home at once and do not bring
along any of your family. Take a few indispensable things. Place yourself
as far as possible from the centre, near the forests the seas or the mountains,
before the whirling motion as it gets stronger from minute to minute begins
to pour in towards the middle, suffocating in ghettoes, closets, basements.
Hang on forcefully to the outer circumference. Keep your head down.
Have your two hands constantly free. Take good care of the muscles of
your legs.

MIROSLAV HOLUB

Suffering

Ugly creatures, ugly grunting creatures,
Completely concealed under the point of the needle,
    behind the curve of the Research Task Graph,
Disgusting creatures with foam at the mouth,
    with bristles on their bottoms,
One after the other
They close their pink mouths
They open their pink mouths
They grow pale
Flutter their legs
    as if they were running a very
    long distance,

They close ugly blue eyes,
They open ugly blue eyes
    and
    they're
    dead.

But I ask no questions,
no one asks any questions.

And after their death we let the ugly creatures
    run in pieces along the white expanse
    of the paper electrophore
We let them graze in the greenish-blue pool
    of the chromatogram
And in pieces we drive them for a dip
    in alcohol
    and xylol
And the immense eye of the ugly animal god
    watches their every move
    through the tube of the microscope

And the bits of animals are satisfied
like flowers in a flower-pot
    like kittens at the bottom of a pond
    like cells before conception.
But I ask no questions,
    no one asks any questions,
Naturally no one asks

Whether these creatures wouldn't have preferred
   to live all in one piece,
   their disgusting life
   in bogs
   and canals,
Whether they wouldn't have preferred to eat
   one another alive,
Whether they wouldn't have preferred to make love
   in between horror and hunger,
Whether they wouldn't have preferred to use
   all their eyes and pores to perceive
   their muddy stinking little world
Incredibly terrified,
Incredibly happy
In the way of matter which can do no more.

But I ask no questions,
   no one asks any questions,
Because it's all quite useless,
Experiments succeed and experiments fail,
Like everything else in this world,
   in which the truth advances
   like some splendid silver bulldozer
   in the tumbling darkness,

Like everything else in this world,
   in which I met a lonely girl
   inside a shop selling bridal veils,

In which I met a general covered
   with oak leaves,
In which I met ambulance men who could find no
   wounded,
In which I met a man who had lost
   his name,
In which I met a glorious and famous, bronze,
   incredibly terrified rat,
In which I met people who wanted to lay down
   their lives and people who wanted to lay down
   their heads in sorrow,
In which, come to think of it, I keep meeting my
   own self at every step.

Death in the Evening

High, high.

Her last words wandered across the ceiling
like clouds.
The sideboard wept.
The apron shivered
as if covering an abyss.

The end. The young ones had gone to bed.

But towards midnight
the dead woman got up,
put out the candles (a pity to waste them),

quickly mended the last stocking,
found her fifty nickels
in the cinnamon tin
and put them on the table,
found the scissors fallen behind the cupboard,
found a glove
they had lost a year ago,
tried all the door knobs,
tightened the tap,
finished her coffee,
and fell back again.

In the morning they took her away.
She was cremated.
The ashes were coarse
as coal.

The Door

Go and open the door.
   Maybe outside there's
   a tree, or a wood,
   a garden,
   or a magic city.

Go and open the door.
   Maybe a dog's rummaging.
   Maybe you'll see a face,
or an eye,
or the picture
         of a picture.

Go and open the door.
   If there's a fog
   it will clear.

Go and open the door.
   Even if there's only
   the darkness ticking,
   even if there's only
   the hollow wind,
   even if
      nothing
         is there,
go and open the door.

At least
there'll be
a draught.

Great and Strong

A little blood, more or less, he said,
He was great and strong, so strong
    it must have been from weakness,
A little blood, he said, and went to wash his hands,
Of course there are things you can't wash off,
But that he didn't know, for he was strong,
He was smart with his elbows, then used his fists,
When he spoke he guzzled the words of others,
The seeing air was stunned and the ant-swarm
    of the transistors crawled through his ears,
A little blood, this man said and
    instantly his words were the thoughts of all,
It was he who conquered at Carthage,
Clean as the map of an unnecessary battle,
Clean as the anatomy of a hyena,
Clean as the conscience of a gun,
Clean as the hands that run a slaughter-house,
Clean as the king of the ants,
Pure as the sperm of Genghis Khan,
Clean as the spore of anthrax,
Clean as the bare behind of death,
All bent their heads,
The tampons bowed to him
And only a little blood
    wept
    on the ground.

Other poems by Holub will be found in the Broadcast Notes for Television Programme 15.

VASKO POPA

From *Games*

The nail

One be the nail another the pincers
The others are workmen

The pincers take the nail by the head
With their teeth with their hands they grip him
And tug him tug
To get him out of the ceiling
Usually they only pull his head off
It's difficult to get a nail out of the ceiling

Then the workmen say
The pincers are no good
They smash their jaws they break their arms
And throw them out of the window

After that someone else be the pincers
Someone else the nail
The others are workmen

Between games

No one is resting,

This one keeps moving his eyes about
Puts them on his shoulders
And willy nilly goes backwards
Puts them on the soles of his feet
And again willy nilly comes back headlong

And this one has turned himself altogether into an ear
And heard everything that can't be heard
But he's had enough
And is aching to turn back into himself
But without eyes he can't see how

And that one has uncovered all his faces
And is chasing them one after the other over the roofs
The last he throws underfoot
And buries his head in his hands

And this one has stretched out his look
Stretched it from thumb to thumb
And is walking along it walking
At first slowly afterwards more quickly
And quicker and quicker

And that one is playing with his head
Tosses it up into the air
And catches it on his forefinger
Or doesn't catch it at all

No one is resting

Ashes

Some are nights others stars

Each night lights up its star
And dances a black dance round it
Until the star burns out

Then the nights split up
Some become stars
The others remain nights

Again each night lights up its star
And dances a black dance round it
Until the star burns out

The last night becomes both star and night
It lights itself
Dances the black dance round itself

From *One bone to another*

At the beginning

That's better
We've got away from the flesh

Now we will do what we will
Say something

Would you like to be
The backbone of a streak of lightning

Say something more

What should I say to you
Pelvis of a storm

Say something else

I don't know anything else
Ribs of the heavens

We are not anyone's bones
Say something different

After the beginning

What shall we do now

Indeed what shall we do
Now we'll have marrow for supper

We ate the marrow for lunch
Now a hollow feeling is nagging at me

Then we'll make music
We like music

What shall we do when the dogs come
They like bones

Then we'll stick in their throats
And have fun

In the sun

It's marvellous sunbathing naked
I never liked the flesh

I wasn't keen on those rags either
I'm crazy about you naked like this

Don't let the sun caress you
Let's rather love each other just the two of us

Only not here only not in the sun
Here everything can be seen bone darling

From *Earth Erect*

The Death of Black George

They cut off his head as he slept
Bore it away to the city of our king cur
And threw it to the whelps

When he awakes he'll go after it
A black handkerchief in his left hand
And a black rose in his right

His wolves will ride out to meet him
On black horses
With black pennons

They'll carry his head
On crossed black flutes
Bound with widows' black braids

His head will shine
Crowned with black beams
Of the black sun

When he awakes

From *Imitation of the Sun*

Blind sun

Two lame sunbeams
Lead the blind sun

Morning is seeking his fortune
On the other side of heaven
He isn't at his own doorstep

Midday has fallen low
He's gadding about with the lightning
He's never at home

Evening has gone out into the world
With his bedding on his back
He's begging on some star

With open arms
Only night has come out
To meet the blind sun

Foreign sun

Whose head did this one-eyed bastard
Drop out of

Who's he gawping at now
Who's he rolling after
Over the fallow heavens

Why is he sizing us up
He'd just love to burn us to cinders

32

As if from down here we
Had doused his rabid father
With cold water

He'd better cool off
Heaven's made a mistake

From *Give me back my rags*

1

Give me back my rags

My rags of pure dreaming
Of silken smiling of striped foreboding
Of my cloth of lace

My rags of spotted hope
Of burnished desire of mottled glances
Of skin from my face

Give me back my rags
Give me whan I ask you nicely

3

I won't take you a pick-a-back
I won't carry you wherever you say

I won't not even shod with gold
Nor harnessed to the wind's three wheeled chariot
Nor bridled with the rainbow's bridle

Don't try to buy me

I won't not even with my feet in my pocket
Nor threaded through a needle nor tied in a knot
Nor reduced to a simple rod

Don't try to scare me

I won't not even grilled nor twice grilled
Neither raw nor salted
I won't not even in a dream

Don't kid yourself
It's not on I won't

11

I've wiped your face off my face
Ripped your shadow off my shadow

Levelled the hills in you
Turned your plains into hills

Set your seasons at odds within you
Turned all the ends of the world from you

Wrapped the path of my life around you
My impenetrable my impossible path

Now you just try to find me

13

Don't try any tricks monster

You hid a knife under your scarf
You stepped over the line you tripped me up
You spoiled the game

That my heaven might turn over
That my sun might smash its head
That my rags might be scattered

Monster don't try any tricks with the monster

Give me back my rags
I'll give you yours

With exception of 'The Death of Black George' from Popa's *Earth Erect* the text of all these poems is from the relevant Penguin selection listed below.

SUGGESTIONS FOR FURTHER STUDY

1   Ted Hughes often suggests that since all the norms have gone one must work at the extremes. Do you see this as a link between him and Popa?

2   How important is the theme of survival in these three East European poets? Trace some of the different ways in which they deal with it.

3   How far do you think the use of surreal images by Popa, or of scientific vocabulary by Holub, is justified?

4   In what way, and to what extent, would you call Herbert and Holub political poets?

5   'There was no greater god at that time [than the god of irony].' (Herbert, 'From Mythology'.) Examine the use made of irony by Herbert and/or Holub.

REFERENCES AND FURTHER READING

Alvarez, A. (1965) *Under Pressure*, Penguin.
Herbert, Zbigniew (trans Czeslaw Milosz and Peter Dale Scott) (1968) *Selected Poems*, Penguin.
Holub, Miroslav (trans Ian Milner and George Theiner) (1967) *Selected Poems*, Penguin.
Holub, Miroslav (trans Ian and Jarmila Milner) (1971) *Although*, Cape.
Popa, Vasko (trans Anne Pennington) (1969) *Selected Poems*, Penguin.
Popa, Vasko (trans Anne Pennington) (1973) *Earth Erect*, Anvil Press.
Theiner, George (ed) (1969) *New Writing in Czechoslovakia*, Penguin.
Wieniewska, Celina (ed) (1967) *Polish Writing Today*, Penguin.

Magazines

Stand, Vol 10 No. 2, 1969 ('New Writing from Czechoslovakia')
Encounter, January 1976 (poems by Holub)
The New Review, February 1976 (poems by Holub)
Modern Poetry in Translation, Nos 1, 5, 7, 17, 23–24, 25 (index)

CONTENTS POETRY IN PUBLIC

1 INTRODUCTION – BACKGROUND

1.1 Poetry has been 'public' for longer than it has been 'private'. It was spoken or sung aloud before it was read in silence. It is in fact much older than writing, older perhaps even than any precise distinction between public and private. Some people have argued that the earliest human speech was rhythmic, the accompaniment of work or dancing; that men 'sang' before they 'spoke'. The question can never be answered because our own distinctions between speech and song cannot be read back into the past without uncertainty. What we can say however is that among simple peoples still surviving today the habit of composing in solitude and singing in company is widespread. Of the Andaman Islanders, for instance, Radcliffe Brown writes:

> A man composes his song as he cuts a canoe or a bow or as he paddles a canoe, singing it over softly to himself until he is satisfied with it. He then awaits an opportunity to sing it in public. (Radcliffe Brown *The Andaman Islanders*, p 132.)

And E. E. Evans-Pritchard says of the Nuer of Africa:

> The Nuer are poetic; most men and women compose songs which are sung at dances and concerts and composed for the creator's own pleasure and chanted by him in lonely pastures . . . Youths break into song, praising their kinsmen, sweet-hearts, and cattle, when they feel happy, wherever they are. (Evans-Pritchard *The Nuer*, p 46.)

These are only two of numerous examples recorded by anthropologists from all over the world.[1]

1.2 The invention of writing adds a new possibility. Not only can poetry be retained from one generation to the next without the aid of memory, so that public performances can be repeated more or less exactly; but the solitary reader can now find the work of someone whom he has never seen or known, and, as it were, communicate with him alone as if he were a friend or a confidant or a lover. Thus a new and intimate relationship is established between writer and reader.

1.3 But the discovery of writing did not simply supersede the performance of poetry in public. And it would be misleading to think of a simple linear development between 'primitive' poetry performed in public and modern poetry read in solitude and silence.

1.4 Over the centuries during which writing and printing have spread, and during which privacy has increased in the home, particularly in Northern Europe and North America, poetry read alone and silently has certainly become the norm; today most people who write poems write for a book, and know that the book will be read, if at all, by a solitary reader. But completely silent reading may be a very recent develop-

---

[1]See Willard Trask, *The Unwritten Song*, 2 vols., Cape, 1969.

ment indeed. Only one instance of silent reading in solitude is recorded in the ancient world; it was noted by St Augustine, who was astonished by it. Children still usually mouth words slowly, under their breath or aloud, when they first learn to read; as late as the last century, it was apparently normal for people reading poetry to themselves still to speak it aloud in the same way.

1.5 There have been a number of other factors delaying the development of poetry towards privacy and silence. One has been music. As far as we know Sappho in the sixth century BC sang or chanted her love poems aloud among her choir of girls. And the further development of writing has not by any means tended to drive out the singing of verse to music: on the contrary, the invention of more accurate forms of notation has given song writing and performance new kinds of stimulus. The influence of music is always tending to bring even the most intimate poetry into public, for performance. The number of people who can read through the score of a song in silence is far fewer than those who can read a text alone with pleasure. Song settings, and poems composed primarily for music, seem to demand performance. And poetry set to music has remained tolerable to people in company, even since, to the English at least, the speaking of verse aloud has often come to seem overwhelmingly embarrassing.

1.6 A second counter-tendency to the privacy of poetry has come from the stage. Particularly in England, where the example of Shakespeare has been so dominant, poets have seldom been able to forget the possibility of dramatic poetry. Yeats, Eliot and Auden among twentieth-century poets have all tried their hand at writing verse drama; and this has been one of the forces that has kept alive a tradition of poetry in public into the twentieth century.

1.7 Radio drama seems specially to favour the interior monologue characteristic of most 'private' poems today. Radio is listened to mainly by audiences of two or one in solitude; and in itself it is doubtful whether it has created a wholly new context for poetry in public, except in the degree to which it has given new emphasis to the sound of the poem read aloud.

1.8 But finally, even the most private poetry has been performed in public at poetry readings. Poets have frequently had to make their living, or make their poems known, by reading in public (often in the United States, where the campus reading tour has long been a form of outdoor relief for the European poet). Some poets, some actors and some other readers have satisfied a demand for hearing poetry aloud. There has probably never been a time over the past century when a few people have not gathered to hear poetry read aloud, either in someone's home, or in a pub, or in a concert hall. But until the last two decades, such readings had seldom attracted large audiences outside the 'middle' and 'upper' classes, and seldom audiences of the young. This was to be the experience of the late 1950s and 1960s.

2 POETRY OF THE 1950s–1960s

2.1 It came about in the first place through an alliance between poets and popular musicians. Poetry and jazz was the combination which brought popular audiences to readings in the late 1950s; and in the mid-sixties the popularity of the Liverpool poets, for instance, followed closely on the popularity of Liverpool music.

2.2 Perhaps the most consistent feature of the poems composed from the late fifties onwards expressly for reading in public is something they have in common with jazz:

departure from the traditional or established forms of 'high art'. Whether this has always been a help is a question that will be raised below; but it is certainly what one should expect. Poets in revolt against both a literary establishment and a social establishment (ten or twenty years ago, that is: perhaps they now form part of both) will naturally have looked to similar spirits as examples in the past: and these ancestors must often have included men who broke with traditional verse forms, because that seemed at the time a way of expressing individual truth and feeling against the restrictions of inherited social convention. In the case of the 'public' poets of the fifties and sixties the ancestors acknowledged were usually Blake – especially his prophetic books – and then mostly Americans: Whitman, Allen Ginsberg, Charles Olson, and behind both Ginsberg and Olson, William Carlos Williams, contemporary and college friend of Ezra Pound.

WILLIAMS AND GINSBERG

2.3 When, in the early years of the century, Pound and Eliot came to London, as the centre of the literary world, William Carlos Williams stayed put in Paterson, New Jersey, working as a doctor. He developed a poetry that celebrated the everyday, in relaxed economical language, close to the vernacular of his home town; his poems have the character of immediate observations rather than products of labour and polishing. He wanted forms of verse in which he could write quickly, between medical tasks. When *The Waste Land* was published he described it as 'wiping out' the world he was creating, and 'returning us to the classroom'. (Williams *Autobiography*.) A similar charge recurs nearly half a century later in the 'Afterwords' to an influential collection of platform poetry, *Children of Albion* (edited by Michael Horovitz) with a title and a cover illustration taken from Blake. Eliot is there cast in the same role – the 'shadow' over young poets, with his demand for erudition before composition.

2.4 The influence of Williams has not been merely critical: it has operated directly on other people's verse. Consider this well-known poem by him.

> *The Red Wheelbarrow*
>
> so much depends
> upon
>
> a red wheel
> barrow
>
> glazed with rain
> water
>
> beside the white
> chickens

Allen Ginsberg also grew up in Paterson, New Jersey, son of a poet. Dr Williams was a family friend. Here is an early poem, written before 'Howl':

> *In back of the real*
>
> railroad yard in San Jose
>   I wandered desolate
> in front of a tank factory
>   and sat on a bench
> near the switchman's shack.

A flower lay on the hay on
      the asphalt highway
– the dread hay flower
      I thought – It had a
brittle black stem and
      corolla of yellowish dirty
spikes like Jesus' inchlong
      crown, and a soiled
dry center cotton tuft
      like a used shaving brush
that's been lying under
      the garage for a year.

Yellow, yellow flower, and
      flower of industry,
tough spikey ugly flower,
      flower nonetheless,
with the form of the great yellow
      Rose in your brain!
This is the flower of the World.

Without talking too much about 'influences', one might say that Ginsberg here seems to be after a similar kind of poetry to Williams's, a redemption of the everyday from insignificance by something like a painter's 'still life', yet without the connotation of painterly detachment that 'stillness' may suggest (which Charles Tomlinson for example, working in this country, has retained).

Figure 1   Allen Ginsberg (Camera Press (H/D) London)

2.5   One of the best poets to have written in this way, among English-born writers, is probably Denise Levertov, who has lived in the United States for many years. Though like most poets she will read her work aloud when asked, she is in no sense a 'platform' poet.

The Rainwalkers

An old man whose black face
shines golden-brown as wet pebbles
under the streetlamp, is walking
two mongrel dogs of dis-
proportionate size, in the rain,
in the relaxed early-evening avenue.

The small sleek one wants to stop,
docile to the imploring soul of the trashbasket,
but the young tall curly one
wants to walk on; the glistening sidewalk
entices him to arcane happenings.

Increasing rain. The old bareheaded man
smiles and grumbles to himself.
The lights change: the avenue's
endless nave echoes notes of
liturgical red. He drifts

between his dogs' desires.
The three of them are enveloped –
turning now to go crosstown – in their
sense of each other, of pleasure,
of weather, of corners,
of leisurely tensions between them
and private silence.

Consider now 'Incident' by Adrian Mitchell, one of the best-known of those English
poets who have read widely in public over the past two decades:

Incident

At Chorley Station on May 30th, 1969, I saw a railwayman
bailing out the signal-box with a pewter mug and pouring
the water inaccurately down into a scarlet wheelbarrow.

The echo of Williams is probably part of the point. This particular poem does not
need – perhaps does not specially benefit from – reading aloud: the appeal is at least
as much to the eye as to the ear.

2.6   When Ginsberg read widely in public, from the late 1950s on, he struck out towards
new forms derived from Biblical rhythms and those of other religious texts, from
Whitman and from Blake's prophetic books. Ginsberg invented from these sources
a long incantatory line of his own. For example,

Psalm III

To God: to illuminate all men. Beginning with Skid Road.
Let Occidental and Washington be transformed into a higher place, the plaza
of eternity.
Illuminate the welders in shipyards with the brilliance of their torches.
Let the crane operator lift up his arm for joy.
Let elevators creak and speak, ascending and descending in awe.
Let the mercy of the flower's direction beckon in the eye.
Let the straight flower bespeak its purpose in straightness – to seek the light.
Let the crooked flower bespeak its purpose in crookedness – to seek the light.
Let the crookedness and straightness bespeak the light.

41

Let Puget Sound be a blast of light.

I feed on your Name like a cockroach on a crumb – this cockroach is holy.

(From *Reality Sandwiches*)

Or again

A Supermarket in California

What thoughts I have of you tonight, Walt Whitman, for I walked down the sidestreets under the trees with a headache self-conscious looking at the full moon.

In my hungry fatigue, and shopping for images, I went into the neon fruit supermarket, dreaming of your enumerations!

What peaches and what penumbras! Whole families shopping at night! Aisles full of husbands! Wives in the avocados, babies in the tomatoes! – and you, Garcia Lorca, what were you doing down by the watermelons?

I saw you, Walt Whitman, childless, lonely old grubber, poking among the meats in the refrigerator and eyeing the grocery boys.

I heard you asking questions of each: Who killed the pork chops? What price bananas? Are you my Angel?

I wandered in and out of the brilliant stacks of cans following you, and followed in my imagination by the store detective.

We strode down the open corridors together in our solitary fancy tasting artichokes, possessing every frozen delicacy, and never passing the cashier.

Where are we going, Walt Whitman? The doors close in an hour. Which way does your beard point tonight?

(I touch your book and dream of our odyssey in the supermarket and feel absurd.)

Will we walk all night through solitary streets? The trees add shade to shade, lights out in the houses, we'll both be lonely.

Will we stroll dreaming of the lost America of love past blue automobiles in driveways, home to our silent cottage?

Ah, dear father, graybeard, lonely old courage-teacher, what America did you have when Charon quit poling his ferry and you got out on a smoking bank and stood watching the boat disappear on the black waters of Lethe?

The debt to Blake and Whitman is not merely one of verse forms. (See Record 1, *Rhythms of Poetry*, OU 21.) There is also in Ginsberg a free use of the idea of holiness, and a determination (by benediction rather than by plain description) once again to redeem the everyday, the despised, and rejected, and to assert its equal holiness with what is officially recognized as sacred. He is perhaps creating a consciousness typical of the manic rather than depressive pole of the mind, in which everything normally despised is accepted and celebrated. (Of course, every poetic style can be imitated without its original driving force, and Ginsbergian benediction can also be parodied by holying any list of objects, parts or functions of the body, without the impetus of his imagination behind it.)

2.7 Ginsberg has had a strong influence on the development of public poetry in Britain. A visit to Oxford in 1958 – where he and Corso read to a group of slightly shocked young poets – seems to have suggested new ways of writing to a number of those who heard him, including the editor of *Children of Albion*, as he records in the 'Afterwords' mentioned above. Ginsberg – he can be seen briefly in the television programme *Poetry in Public* – was the dominating presence at the first of the two Albert Hall poetry festivals in the mid-sixties, where 'platform' poetry first seems to have reached the attention of a very large public. His example has probably had some effect on all those poets who have written expressly for performance in public since the 1950s.

2.8   One of the best known of these, in Britain, is Brian Patten. He began reading in the mid-sixties, while still in his teens. You can either listen to, or read for yourself, one of his poems, 'Party Piece', on the first record *Rhythms of Poetry*, where it is read by Patrick Garland. Brian Patten also reads three of his poems in the television programme, *Poetry in Public*: the text of these – 'The Projectionist's Nightmare', 'A Small Dragon' and 'Portrait of a Young Girl Raped at a Suburban Party' – can be found in the Broadcast Notes to that programme.

3   CRITICAL ISSUES: 'TOBY BELCH VERSUS MALVOLIO'?

3.1   Brian Patten's work has aroused violent controversy. An examination of this controversy, and also of the reception of the anthology *Children of Albion*, may provide some elements for a consideration of this kind of poetry in general. Critical decisions about the poems themselves can of course be taken only by each individual reader for himself or herself.

3.2   To some critics, Brian Patten's work is not poetry at all. Donald Davie published a very angry review of Philip Larkin's *Oxford Book of Twentieth Century English Verse*,[2] criticizing the editor for including 'Portrait of a Young Girl Raped at a Suburban Party', which he quoted in full. 'How Patten got to the point of thinking that this sort of thing was a poem is a good and appalling question', wrote Davie. 'At no point, by no one of the many ways available, has imagination entered, penetrated, opened up, transformed . . . The piece is pathetically implausible and ineffective.' And he asked how Larkin brought himself 'to present us with this artlessness . . . as what we should take some pride in, as representing us to posterity'. He called Larkin – as anthologist – 'a man who thinks that poetry is a private indulgence, or a professional entertainer's patter or, at most, a symptom for social historians to brood over.' By contrast, wrote Davie, poetry is 'to some of us . . . a *calling*: our commitment . . . however far we are from practising it full-time, is not wholly unlike a religious vocation, or the vocation of a nurse: we feel we have heard a call, which we try to respond to.'

3.3   There was a succession of letters in reply. Readers pointed[2] out that similar doubts could be felt about other modern poems, even one by as fine a poet as Davie himself;[3] while as for a sense of calling, Larkin's own poetry not only gave evidence of 'vocation' but actually included a poem about Larkin's sense of 'calling' which sounded uncannily like Davie's own concept:

>   What calls me is that lifted rough-tongued bell
>   (Art, if you like) whose individual sound
>   Insists I too am individual.
>   It speaks, I hear.

Larkin confined his own replies to saying that he stood by the choices he had made and had made them himself.[4] But in an interview given at the time he suggested a conception of his task as anthologist that was not obviously less serious than Davie's.

[2] *The Listener*, 30 March 1973.
[3] *The Listener*, 12 April, 19 April 1973.
[4] *The Listener*, 5 April, 17 May 1973.

He said that he had decided he should ignore no book of poems produced in his period, and should give as much attention to the neglected as to the already known. 'In simplistic terms', as he put it in his interview with Anthony Thwaite[5], 'I read all the poetry produced in this century, which took about four and a half years, and then picked out the bits I liked the best.' And in 1975, in an interview for Radio Programme 16, *Modernism and Tradition*, Larkin confirmed his choice: presented with the familiar pattern of English verse in this century as two streams originating with Hardy and Pound, he accepted it, but picked out the popular poets like Patten as a third group:

> They are writing and reading very simple poems which I think are under-valued . . . When I read them I think, 'Yes that's a perfectly good emotion, it's quite well expressed.' . . . I'd sooner see people concerning themselves with that kind of poem than with the heavily cerebral, heavily referential poems that tend to get more respect in the universities.

So fundamentally do Davie and Larkin differ on the question of Patten's poetry that Davie seems to have been unable to believe Larkin actually liked Patten's work, and judged it to be good.

Figure 2   Brian Patten (Courtesy of George Allen & Unwin)

3.4   'Artless' is of course a two-edged term of abuse and Davie is unlikely to mean simply that Patten's poems *sound* artless. A poem can sound artless without *being* artless; this is so ancient and agreed a judgement of all ages that it would surely be parochial if one felt that in the twentieth century alone poetry ought to show the swollen veins and sweating forehead of its composition. Perhaps some readers, and even some poets, have felt this in the twentieth century. But this is surely not what Davie can be saying: he must mean that good poetry should not *be* artless, however much its art may be of the kind 'that conceals art'.

[5] *The Listener*, 12 April 1973.

3.5 Even then, however, a poem, like any work of art, may arrive in literally any way, including effortlessly. This can seem horrible to those who place the highest value in work. Marx for example defined work at one point in his writing by instancing musical composition as the clearest example. He described it as 'in the most damned earnest, the most intensive effort'.[6] And this applies to Beethoven perfectly. But it is not clear that it applies to Mozart, whose ease of composition – after a good meal, or when travelling in a carriage – is recorded delightfully in his correspondence. One can never know how a work of art will originate, and one cannot define its quality, even its technical craftsmanship, by reference to the degree of effort or sense of vocation experienced by the artist. Otherwise the whole matter of art would be capable of being regulated like a savings bank or an examination, which it demonstrably is not.

3.6 However, there is a special reason why the poems of Patten and his friends may have been attacked for 'artlessness'. Many of the poems associated with public readings in the last two decades have been primarily poems written for the ear and the performing voice, even – and this is a more serious limitation – for the particular performing voice of the poet. A. Alvarez reviewing the anthology *Children of Albion* in *The Observer*[7] put the point strongly:

> The verse can't exist without the writer who speaks it, not because he adds subtleties the reader will miss but because his physical presence compounds embarrassment: if you see him there, delivering the stuff, it's hard to be properly contemptuous; instead, you feel ashamed for him, and sorry.

He also said:

> Where genuinely *avant-garde* artists take the violence of their time into their own selves and make their art painfully out of that, Horovitz's circus of neo-Blakean neo-pop celebrants hope to bring about a revolution by denying social realities and substituting a vague, wistful benevolence, all flowers, hash and polymorphous free love . . . [Their poetry] makes no demands, it covers them from the harsh world . . . But it has nothing, nothing at all, to do with the real thing, the demanding, heart-breaking, unforgiving craft of poetry.

But perhaps just as the song lyric is a different kind of poem from the poem on the page, and must – if it is to be any good as a song – have another kind of craftsmanship, so the poem that is designed primarily for reading aloud may have to be different from poetry written primarily for the page. Possibly it should be printed differently, as songs are: for otherwise there is genuine danger of confusing the reader and perhaps the young – children in schools perhaps being encouraged in 'creative writing' classes to compose laboriously and silently, on the page, imitations of some 'platform poem' that, as solemnly published, is no more than a rough indication of the effect for the ear, like the often banal printed melodic line from which a jazz improvisation starts. I personally feel this about a number of the contributions to *Children of Albion*: sometimes a mere approximate indication of what the writer's voice will do has there been printed in just the same way as a poem written for the page.

3.7 This cannot however explain all the differences between the one group of critics and the other over the work of the 'platform' poets. Larkin, for example, cannot have chosen Patten's poems merely for the sound of them performed in Patten's voice; at the time when he first heard him reading in public he had already included him in his unpublished selection. (He mentioned the point in conversation at the reading.)

[6]Marx, *Grundrisse*.
[7]9 November 1969.

3.8 Perhaps a more central reason for the critical division about Patten and his colleagues – and for the violence of its tone – is the question of publicity. Over the past few decades, the paperback and above all television have profoundly changed the relationship between certain writers and the public. The 'platform' poets, though they did not begin as public figures, have appealed to large audiences at readings and through the mass media. Since poetry is so much a matter of private communication, and since the demands of crowds and mass media salesmanship are so often enemies of precision, of honesty and of the communication of individual truth, there is every reason for approaching with caution poetry that is 'plugged' by these means. It could be very much like the large-scale selling of patriotic poetry at the beginning of the First World War, through the then dominant media of press and pulpit, while the private poets of protest and individual truth – largely unknown to the public – were saying infinitely more important things. (Both Arnold Kettle and Jon Stallworthy described this situation: Units 4–5 *Modernism and Its Origins*, Part 2 and Radio Programme 3, *The Poetry of the First World War*.)

3.9 But caution and condemnation are not the same. New poetry is always surprising: certainly always surprising to the poet who writes it; and neither reader nor poet can know where the next good poem is coming from, or through whom. It seems to me – though I am not a professional critic – that it is perhaps worth recalling the first poem read by Miroslav Holub, 'Dialogue with a Poet', in Television Programme 15. (Incidentally, it was Alvarez who introduced Holub's poetry to this country in a fine Penguin collection.) To Holub – a scientist and a poet – his uncertainty about the next poem, even his own next poem, was the one thing he could be quite certain of.

3.10 Where I think a critic might perform a genuinely helpful service would be in pointing out the possibility of neglected alternatives to his contemporaries, in verse forms above all. In particular, there seems to be a horror of traditional forms, on the part of most of the platform poets, which strikes me as paradoxical. In songwriting the elements of traditional English versification are in no way obstacles to expression, but functional and timeless; but most of those poets who speak their poems aloud on platforms seem to want to be revolutionary in two ways at once. On the one hand they want to bring poetry off the page and make it an oral art again; on the other, as we suggested above, they naturally ally themselves with poets who have wanted to make 'revolutions' in their own time, in particular with those who have wanted to explode the traditional elements of metre, stanza form, rhyme, and concentrated language. Thus they tend to feel affinities with Blake, Whitman and Lawrence, and also, as far as certain surface aspects of versification are concerned – the breaking up of the pentameter, for example, but not always the compression this was intended to produce – with Pound and the 'modernists'. I would not want to argue about how anyone else 'ought to' write. But it seems to me that the more you want a poem to stand up away from the page, the less use to you are highly sophisticated free forms developed in the twentieth century on the page and for the page, often dependent on the typewriter and its spacing.

3.11 The American poet Charles Olson took the opposite point of view in his 'Projective Verse' (1950). He wrote there that the typewriter was a way of giving poetry back to the ear because it allowed the poet for the first time to indicate to any reader, silent 'or otherwise', by precise spacing, his intervals of breathing and the exact nature of all his rhythms. In a radio interview the year before he died he confirmed this view in general, and said that he considered his own poems on the page to be no more than musical scores, having their true being only when read aloud.[8] However, I disagree perhaps not for American but for English speech. Far from rhyme and metre being 'page-bred' forms, I think they are the natural means that European languages have developed for carrying words to the ear. Print, type and silent reading, by

[8]Alasdair Clayre, *The Poetry of Charles Olson*, BBC Third Programme, 26 August 1969.

46

contrast, have allowed free forms to develop, and indeed have come to require them, since after a certain point of a tradition a familiar form that sounds natural when sung or spoken can seem unnecessarily obtrusive, like ruled lines below a child's handwriting, when viewed on the page.

3.12 Free verse forms have also depended largely on hidden relationships to known regular rhythms from the past: as Eliot said, 'the ghost of some simple metre lurking behind the arras even in the free-est verse; to advance menacingly as we doze, and withdraw as we rouse.' The attempt to use free verse consciously to appeal to non-literary audiences is surprising; half the force of free verse is gone. This is not a rule – there are no rules in poetry. But it seems likely that from this beginning a tendency may emerge towards forms so tenuous as to be imperceptible by ear to most new listeners; and poetry may become actually indistinguishable from – not a formal representation of – unorganized thought, the poet himself posed as work of art.

Figure 3   Adrian Mitchell (Photo: Adam Ritchie/Town Camera Press (TAI) London)

3.13 Not all the 'public' poets have written exclusively in free forms. Look back to the poem by Adrian Mitchell 'Incident' quoted on p 41, and at the poem about Norman Morrison quoted by Arnold Kettle in Units 21–22 *Poetry and Politics* p 36; and now look at Adrian Mitchell's 'Hear the Voice of the Critic':

> *Hear the Voice of the Critic*
>
> There are too many colours.
> The Union Jack's all right, selective,
> Two basic colours and one negative,
> Reasonable, avoids confusion.
>   (Of course I respect the red, white and blue)

But there are too many colours.
The rainbow, well it's gaudy, but I am
Bound to admit, a useful diagram
When treated as an optical illusion.
   (Now I'm not saying anything against rainbows)

But there are too many colours.
Take the sea. Unclassifiable.
The sky – the worst offender of all,
Tasteless as Shakespeare, especially at sunset.
   (I wish my body were all one colour).

There are too many colours.
I collect flat white plates.
You ought to see my flat white plates.
In my flat white flat I have a perfect set,
   (It takes up seven rooms).

There are too many colours.

In the first case – 'Incident' – Mitchell was writing almost entirely visual poetry, and there was no need for reading aloud. But elsewhere – as in the other two examples – where he has wanted to compose primarily for the ear, Mitchell has tended to use quite different models: rhythms from jazz, popular songs, from nursery rhymes or sometimes from the English nonsense tradition of Lear and Carroll.

3.14   The last poem is also a reminder that several of the 'platform' writers have made a point of publicizing the critical fury they have aroused, seeing it as the consequence of a struggle between themselves as children of natural impulse, and their critics as academic, inhibited spoilsports. Scorn for carefulness in life and in poetry, and contempt for critics as such, is a theme of several of the poems in the anthology *Children of Albion* referred to earlier. Here is a short poem from that book by Pete Brown:

Reckless

Last night I was reckless –
didn't brush my teeth
and went to bed tasting
my dinner all night

And it tasted good.

One further possible reason for the violence of the controversy between such poets, and critics like Davie and Alvarez, may be worth considering. Perhaps in an age – this is not the first – when different generations have almost different private languages, it is particularly hard for people of different generations to distinguish between poetry that merely uses the unselfconscious speech of its writer and poetry that chooses intentionally crude language or that does not choose with any care for words at all. In the Patten poems above, Larkin presumably saw the first possibility, and Davie the second. Larkin has an extraordinary ear for idiomatic variations and for the English of different classes; as anyone who listens to his own reading of 'Mr Bleaney' (in Radio Programme 14) will no doubt notice. But this is not a simple matter of 'class', for it could be argued that the language of Patten's poems is not at all 'working class' speech. On the contrary, it seems to be in the literary lingua franca of a generation which, through pop lyrics, children's stories, comics and fantasies like those of Tolkien, seems to have accepted, perhaps rather easily, a great deal of the 'poetical' and of the 'fairy tale' into its diction. Since so much of the work of twentieth-century poets has been devoted to avoiding echoes of the poetry of the past, or anything that could be called sentimentality, it is natural and right that critics will object if they find any tendency towards either in the work of a poet. He may however be reflecting the way he himself speaks, or the language of the people he lives among and talks to, and this is also something that most twentieth-century poets have wanted to do. The critical requirements may be contradictory.

3.15 The violent division between two schools of critics and poets in the nineteen-sixties seemed at one point to create a danger that their postures might become fixed, as 'Toby Belches of the platform versus Malvolios of the printed page'. One side might be cut off from access to the traditional resources of English versification, and to its standards of craftsmanship; while the other would not feel the quickening of enthusiasm and perhaps even of invention that contact with a living audience can bring, not only to the 'platform poet' but to the most formal, hard-working and craftsmanlike one who usually composes for the solitary reader.

4 'PUBLIC' AND 'PRIVATE'

4.1 However, at a festival like the Cambridge one of 1975, recorded in the television programme *Poetry in Public*, not merely 'underground' writers, but many other poets read aloud, and for some listeners it was the older poets like Sorley MacLean, and the middle generation (Ted Hughes and Charles Tomlinson, to say nothing of Holub) who reached the audience most clearly. Yet without the work of Horovitz and the Poets' Co-operative, or Johnnty Boulting with his New Moon Phalène in the mid-sixties, it is unlikely that large popular festivals of poetry like the Cambridge one ten years later would ever have been started.

4.2 The incursion of these poets into the literary world of the nineteen-sixties seems to me therefore to have been beneficial: it set 'standing water' moving. To some extent I agree with Donald Hall. 'In modern art anarchy has proved preferable to the restrictions of a benevolent tyranny. It is preferable as a permanent condition.' (*Contemporary American Poetry* p 25.) The 'platform' poets arrived at a time when poetry was greeted by so little direct response from any public who actually seemed to enjoy it that its publication had come to resemble an examination submitted to the critics, or perhaps the composition by the poet for himself, laboriously, of an epitaph for his own gravestone. Who knows; perhaps the orthodoxy is now Liverpool and the time has come for rebellion in another direction.

4.3 It was Stevie Smith rather than Allen Ginsberg who was probably the central figure at the second Albert Hall poetry reading in the mid-sixties (1966), and she deserves particular attention in this context, because her work seems to bridge the gap between the two worlds of private and public poems. Stevie Smith was a poet and novelist who had long been writing without a wide public, though always highly appreciated by a few critics and readers. She had developed her own way of performing in public, which was a half-singing, half-chanting recital. But she remained a poet of the private voice, perhaps almost of the shared private joke.

4.4 And the tone of the shared private joke may be the key to a great deal of what has been read on public platforms in the last decade. Stevie Smith's poems were generally greeted by laughter mixed with applause when she read them. What she has in common with some of the 'platform' poets, as with Betjeman, even with Larkin sometimes (see 'The Card-Players' reprinted in Unit 28 p 33), is a way of writing a poem that includes tones in which English people tell each other jokes, often to say something perfectly serious which, for some reason, may not be possible for that particular poet to say without embarrassment in England. Sometimes such poems can liberate from prose standards of sense and solemnity, and make possible surrealistic juxtapositions of imagery. And perhaps as with Christopher Smart in the

Figure 4 Stevie Smith (Camera Press BRO/CO London)

eighteenth century[9] it will turn out that those who have written outside the strict canons of normal seriousness in their period may be particularly enjoyed, and read seriously, by future generations. In any case, here are two examples of Stevie Smith's work:

I Remember

It was my bridal night I remember,
An old man of seventy-three
I lay with my young bride in my arms,
A girl with t.b.
It was wartime, and overhead
The Germans were making a particularly heavy raid on Hampstead.
What rendered the confusion worse, perversely
Our bombers had chosen that moment to set out for Germany.
Harry, do they ever collide?
I do not think it has ever happened,
Oh my bride, my bride.

[9]See Record 1 *Rhythms of Poetry*, OU 21.

Lady 'Rogue' Singleton

Come, wed me, Lady Singleton,
And we will have a baby soon
And we will live in Edmonton
Where all the friendly people run.

I could never make you happy darling,
Or give you the baby you want,
I would always very much rather, dear,
Live in a tent.

I am not a cold woman, Henry,
But I do not feel for you,
What I feel for the elephants and the miasmas
And the general view.

FOLKSONGS AND ORAL POETRY

4.5   A longer essay might have said more about two neighbouring fields. One is 'concrete poetry', poetry where words are reduced to their elements – either to sounds or to letters on the page – and made into new patterns for the ear or the eye. A little of this was shown in the television programme *Poetry in Public*. The other is songs. Pop songs are already well known through the mass media and nothing need be added about them here; but the singers and writers who have worked in the less publicized world of the folksong clubs have played a part in the revival of 'oral' poetry; apart from a crop of writers in traditional forms, the folksong revival has produced singers like Martin Carthy who have contributed to the ballad tradition.[10]

4.6   In songs, the streams of public and private poetry have never been divided. The modern European art of lyrical poetry stems particularly from early medieval Provence, where the song was the normal form of poetry. Many surviving medieval English lyrics are clearly song texts, to accompany music or dancing; and the Elizabethan plays – like Elizabethan life – are full of songs. It is only with the coming of more formally elaborate music, where the simple melody line is lost in the complexity of composition, that a separation between words and music takes place: at first in the polyphonic music of the middle ages; then, after a revival of the simple song in the Renaissance, again in all branches of music but folksong in England, about the turn of the eighteenth century. Elsewhere in Europe some of the finest poets continued to write texts for great composers, as Dryden still wrote for Purcell. But in England the 'art song', in which a text often not originally composed for music was tortured into subservience to an overriding musical pattern, was at best a musical rather than a poetic form. There was a brief revival of poets' songs in the late eighteenth and early nineteenth centuries; in Scotland with Burns, and in England and Anglo-Ireland with Byron and his friend Tom Moore. But the twentieth century did not inherit a flourishing indigenous song tradition. It had to be consciously revived.

4.7   Yeats, towards the end of his life, was working hard at plans to 'resore the art of English song', and he took the leading part in the publishing of the *Cuala Broadsides* (1936 and 1937). For these a number of poets, himself included, wrote new words to traditional tunes or to newly composed music in traditional forms. Some of his own earlier lyrics, like the popular 'Down by the Salley Gardens', had already been

---

[10]For example Martin Carthy's version of 'The Fair Flower of Serving Men', which derives from fragments printed by Sir Walter Scott, has a central section which turns out to have been written by the singer himself and yet joins seamlessly to produce a new ballad.

written on these lines. Some of his colleague James Stephens's lyrics, such as 'She Moved Through the Fair' have gone into oral tradition among the tinkers and folk-singers of Ireland.

4.8 Ezra Pound was also deeply concerned with music. He wrote an opera (*Villon*), and a treatise on music; and in one of his cantos he does a pastiche seventeenth-century lyric, and dedicates it to Henry Lawes, with a prayer for the revival of the art of English song. And Auden worked on parallel lines in his own way. He was aware of the success of Brecht in writing ballad-like lyrics in Germany with immediate appeal, for the music of Kurt Weill and Hanns Eisler. He was also deeply interested in the Elizabethan lute-songs, and in particular in the lyrics and theories of Thomas Campion, who wrote both words and music of some of the best songs in English, and also a work about prosody that Auden greatly liked.

4.9 Auden set out consciously to write formal lyrics for music, realizing that this involved a quite different form of versification from poetry on the printed page. Elizabethan song writers had believed that a composer should know not only the formal art of music, but the folksong melodies of his own country, as these were likely to suit the rhythms of his own language particularly. Auden wrote a number of song lyrics in folksong metres, as well as jazz-rhythmed poems in the Brechtian manner like 'Victor'. Thus both Yeats and Auden went to folksong for certain of their forms – Auden always somewhat ironically, Yeats without reservation.

4.10 Since then it has proved almost impossible, without strain, to adhere to a wholly local tradition, unaffected by the new developments of the twentieth century; and other writers have been concerned to find rhythms natural to their generation as well as to their language and country. Nevertheless, Yeats and Vaughan Williams, Cecil Sharp and A. L. Lloyd set something moving in the folksong revival which in its own way has made for a new kind of poetry in public; poetry written and sung unambiguously for the ear, and generally away from the large platform and the crowded public hall, as well as away from the cash register. Most poetry has lived away from these.

FURTHER READING

Grevel Lindop 'The Liverpool Poets' in Michael Schmidt and Grevel Lindop (eds) (1972) *British Poetry since 1960: A Critical Survey*, Carcarnet Press.

Adrian Mitchell, 'Poetry Explodes', *The Listener*, 14 May 1970, pp 642–3.

Donald Davie, 'Larkin's Choice', Review of *Oxford Book of Twentieth-Century English Verse*, *The Listener*, 29 March 1973.

REFERENCES

Brown, Radcliffe (1948) *The Andaman Islanders*, Glencoe.

Evans-Pritchard, E. E. (1940) *The Nuer*, Oxford University Press.

Ginsberg, Allen (1956) *Howl and Other Poems*, City Lights Books.

Ginsberg, Allen (1963) *Reality Sandwiches*, City Lights Books.

Hall, Donald (1971) (2nd ed) *Contemporary American Poetry*, Penguin.

Horovitz, Michael (ed) (1969) *Children of Albion*, Penguin.

Mitchell, Adrian (1969) *Out Loud*, Jonathan Cape.

Olson, Charles (1950) 'Projective Verse' in *Poetry New York*, No. 3. Reprinted in Charles Olson (1966) *Selected Writings*, New Directions, pp 15–30, especially pp 22–3.

Penguin Modern Poets (1967) *Williams, Levertov and Rexroth*, Penguin.

Smith, Stevie (1975) *Collected Poems*, Allen Lane.

Williams, W. C. (1951) *Autobiography*, Random House.

ACKNOWLEDGEMENTS

Grateful acknowledgement is made to the following sources for material used in this unit:

Pete Brown, 'Reckless', Fulcrum Press, reprinted in Michael Horowitz (ed), *Children of Albion*, Penguin, 1969; Allen Ginsberg, 'Psalm III' in *Reality Sandwiches*, copyright © 1963 Allen Ginsberg, reprinted by permission of City Lights Books; Allen Ginsberg, 'A Supermarket in California', 'In Back of the Real' in *Howl and Other Poems*, copyright © 1956, 1959 Allen Ginsberg, reprinted by permission of City Lights Books; Zbigniew Herbert, 'Elegy of Fortinbras', translated Czeslaw Milosz, *Encounter*, August 1961; Zbigniew Herbert, 'A Knocker', 'Apollo and Marsyas', 'Our Fear' and 'Pebble', and extracts from 'Jonah', 'Practical Recommendations in the event of a Catastrophe', 'Report from Paradise' from *Selected Poems*, translated Czeslaw Milosz and Peter Dale Scott, Penguin Modern European Poets, 1968, copyright © 1968 Czeslaw Milosz and Peter Dale Scott; Zbigniew Herbert, 'From Mythology', translated Czeslaw Milosz, *The Observer*, 2 September 1962; Miroslav Holub, 'In the Microscope', 'A Helping Hand', 'Suffering', 'Death in the Evening', 'Great and Strong', and 'The Door' from *Selected Poems*, translated Ian Milner and George Theiner, Penguin Modern European Poets, 1967, copyright © 1967 Miroslav Holub, translation copyright © 1967 Penguin Books Ltd; Extract from Miroslav Holub, 'Bullfight' in *Although*, translated Ian and Jarmila Milner, Jonathan Cape, 1971; Miroslav Holub, 'Brief thoughts on cracks', translated Ian Milner (read at a University of Cambridge Poetry Symposium 1976); Denise Levertov, 'The Rainwalkers' in *The Jacobs Ladder*, Jonathan Cape; Adrian Mitchell, 'Incident' from *Ride the Nightmare*, and 'Hear the Voice of the Critic' from *Out Loud*, Jonathan Cape; Vasko Popa, 'St Sava's Forge', 'The Death of Black George' and 'Belgrade' in *Earth Erect*, translated Anne Pennington, Anvil Press Poetry, 1973; Vasko Popa, 'Between Games', 'Ashes', 'Pig', 'The Nail', 'Once upon a time', 'Blind Sun', 'Foreign Sun', 'No. 3', 'No. 10', 'No. 13', 'No. 1', 'No. 8', 'At the Beginning', 'In the Sun', 'After the Beginning' and extract from 'At the End' in *Selected Poems*, translated Anne Pennington, Penguin Books, 1969, reprinted by permission of Olwyn Hughes; Extract from Vasko Popa, 'The Little Box' in 'The Little Box' cycle, *Chapman*, Vol. II, No. 4, 1973, Chapman Publications, Hamilton, Lanarkshire; Extract from R. M. Rilke, 'The Ninth Elegy' from *Duino Elegies*, translated J. B. Leishman, reprinted by permission of St John's College, Oxford and The Hogarth Press; Stevie Smith, 'I remember' and 'Lady "Rogue" Singleton' in *Selected Poems*, Allen Lane, reprinted by permission of the author's literary executor, James MacGibbon; William Carlos Williams, 'The Red Wheelbarrow' in *Collected Earlier Poems*, copyright 1938 New Directions Publishing Corporation, reprinted by permission.

TWENTIETH CENTURY POETRY

Unit 1	English Poetry in 1912
Units 2–3	Thomas Hardy
Units 4–5	Modernism and Its Origins
Unit 6	Ezra Pound
Units 7–8	T. S. Eliot's Poetry 1909–25
Unit 9	T. S. Eliot: Criticism
Units 10–11	T. S. Eliot's Poetry 1926–43
Unit 12	Poetry in Translation
Unit 13	Guillaume Apollinaire
Units 14–17	W. B. Yeats
Units 18–19	William Empson and F. R. Leavis
Unit 20	R. M. Rilke *Duino Elegies*
Units 21–22	Poetry and Politics
Units 23–24	W. H. Auden
Unit 25	Hugh MacDiarmid
Unit 26	Dylan Thomas
Unit 27	Robert Lowell
Unit 28	Philip Larkin
Unit 29	Ted Hughes Sylvia Plath
Unit 30	Robert Graves John Betjeman
Unit 31	Donald Davie Charles Tomlinson Geoffrey Hill
Unit 32	East European Poets Poetry in Public